BOOK ANALYSIS

By Verity Roat

Maurice
BY E. M. FORSTER

E. M. FORSTER

ENGLISH NOVELIST, SHORT STORY WRITER, ESSAYIST AND LIBRETTIST

- **Born in Marylebone (England) in 1879.**
- **Died in Coventry (England) in 1970.**
- **Notable works:**
  - *A Room with a View* (1908), novel
  - *Howards End* (1910), novel
  - *A Passage to India* (1924), novel

Forster was the only child of Alice Clara "Lily" (née Whichelo) and Edward Morgan Llewellyn Forster, an architect, who died when Forster was two years old. In 1883, he and his mother moved to Rooks Nest in Hertfordshire, which later served as the model for Howards End in his novel of the same name. From 1897 to 1901 he attended King's College Cambridge, where he was a member of the Apostles discussion society, which met in secret to debate philosophy. He was a conscientious objector to World War I and travelled to Egypt, Germany and India in

1914. Forster was homosexual, but this was only known by his close friends. He had a long-term relationship with a married policeman, Benjamin Buckingham, and when he died of a stroke aged 91, his ashes were mixed with Buckingham's and scattered in the cemetery in Coventry. Forster published five novels during his lifetime; although he had written *Maurice* some 60 years beforehand, he asked that it only be published after his death due to the homosexual relationship at the centre of the novel. He never finished his seventh novel, *Arctic Summer*.

MAURICE

A HOMOSEXUAL BILDUNGSROMAN (COMING OF AGE STORY)

- **Genre:** novel
- **Reference edition:** Forster, E. M. (2005) *Maurice*. London: Penguin Classics.
- **1st edition:** 1971
- **Themes:** gender and sexuality, homosexuality, class, education, religion, societal expectations, love and relationships, public and private life

Dismissed as "the least satisfactory of all Forster's novels" (King, 1978, cited in Symondson, 2016), *Maurice* tells the story of the titular character's exploration of his homosexuality during his formative years. The novel starts by exploring Maurice Hall's first encounters with sexuality at school, then follows him through his university days where he meets his first homosexual lover, Clive Durham. After university, Clive claims to have become heterosexual and marries a woman. Maurice is devastated, but soon starts a relationship with Clive's gamekeeper. The novel ends happily, with the two agreeing to start a new life together.

Despite having shown the novel to a select group of friends and homosexuality having been legalised in 1967, Forster decided against publishing the novel during his lifetime and instead asked that it be published posthumously. This is because he believed it to be unpublishable, due to public attitudes towards same-sex love.

SUMMARY

SCHOOL DAYS

The novel opens with Maurice Hall, aged 14, walking with his prep-school teacher, Mr Ducie, after an afternoon tea party. Spurred on by Maurice's upcoming progression to Sunnington (a public school), Mr Ducie feels it is his duty to educate Maurice, whose father died some years ago, about sex, women and marriage. Maurice feels disconnected from this conversation, as he does not see marriage with a woman as the ultimate goal of his life and, as such, the reader is given a glimpse into Maurice's internal struggles with his sexuality. His days at Sunnington pass quickly in the space of a handful of pages and end with Maurice receiving a prize on his final day of school. His neighbour, Dr Barry, is present that day and asks Maurice about his plans for the future; Maurice somewhat downheartedly assumes he will follow in his father's footsteps by going to Cambridge and then entering into the stockbroker business.

CAMBRIDGE

At Cambridge, Maurice quickly falls into a routine of spending time with fellow former pupils from Sunnington. He is invited to a lunch party with the Dean, Chapman (one of his school friends) and a relative of the Dean, Risley. Although Maurice is initially unsure how he feels about Risley, he decides to go to his rooms to visit him. Maurice is disappointed when he arrives and finds that Risley is out. However, he meets friend of Risley's instead, Clive Durham. He soon strikes up a friendship with Clive, who recommends that he read Plato's *Symposium,* an ancient Greek work about same-sex love, over the Christmas vacation. When Clive first announces his attraction to Maurice, Maurice is shocked and disgusted. He reacts as society would and shuns Clive, who in turn is heartbroken and refuses to speak to Maurice. Maurice comes to terms with his feelings for Clive and returns to him to tell him that he loves him. The two then enter into a committed relationship, though Clive does not want to physically consummate the relationship.

LIFE AFTER CAMBRIDGE

Shortly after beginning his love affair with Clive, Maurice is 'sent down' (excluded, either temporarily or permanently) from Cambridge, because he skipped several lectures to spend time with Clive. His mother receives a letter from the Dean demanding that Maurice apologise before he will be allowed to return to college. Because of his sense of pride, he is initially reluctant to do this, but when Clive tells him he will be staying on at Cambridge for a fourth year, Maurice decides to apologise so that they can spend the year together. Once they have graduated from Cambridge, Maurice takes a job at his late father's stockbroker firm. Clive becomes a lawyer and invites Maurice to spend every Wednesday night and many weekends with him in his city flat. After several years, Clive falls ill with influenza and during his illness, he believes he has been 'cured' of his homosexuality.

CLIVE AND MAURICE'S SEPARATION

After he has recovered from his illness, Clive tells Maurice that he no longer loves him and decides to embark on a holiday to Greece.

Whilst in Greece, he meets Lady Anne Woods and becomes engaged to her. Because Clive has become distant from Maurice, Maurice discovers this engagement through his mother reading the announcement in the newspaper. Because of this, Maurice decides that he wants to 'cure' himself of his homosexual desires and contacts a man, Mr Lasker Jones, whom a college friend has mentioned. He agrees to stay with Clive and his new wife at his country estate while secretly receiving this cure.

SCUDDER

Maurice attends his first appointment with Mr Lasker Jones, during which he attempts to hypnotise Maurice to rid him of his homosexual desires. Although he feels that this initial meeting has gone well, he returns to Clive's house feeling tormented by his sexuality. He cannot sleep that night and cries out for Clive to come to him. Clive's under-gamekeeper, Alec Scudder, overhears this and assumes that he is being called, so he sneaks into Maurice's room and they 'share' together (have sexual intercourse). Maurice is ashamed at his inability to control his urges and returns home to avoid Scudder and Clive. Scudder is hurt by Maurice's actions and sends him a series of increasingly threatening letters, which make Maurice believe that Scudder is going to call the police on him.

THE BRITISH MUSEUM

Maurice agrees to meet Scudder in London at the British Museum. The two initially argue, but Maurice quickly realises that he has fallen in love with Scudder and vice versa. Scudder is planning to emigrate to Argentina, but Maurice asks him not to, saying he will give up his financial and social position to be with him. Scudder leads Maurice to believe that he still intends to leave, so Maurice goes to wave him off from the dock, but discovers he has missed his passage. Maurice returns to Clive's country estate, hoping to find Scudder at the boathouse, where Scudder had previously suggested they meet. Scudder is in fact there, having sent Maurice a letter to his family home, explaining that he had decided to stay in England. The novel ends happily with the implication that the two enter into a harmonious relationship. In the last chapter, Maurice returns to Clive to tell him about his relationship with Scudder. Clive is appalled and the two never speak again.

CHARACTER STUDY

MAURICE HALL

Despite being a Cambridge graduate, Maurice is a fairly ordinary young man with an unexceptional intellect. He is described as handsome with very dark hair. He has a reasonably loving relationship with his mother and sisters, though he often believes himself to be more important than the latter two (his father having died in his childhood). From early on in his youth, Maurice realises that he is not like other boys, in that he seemingly has no interest in women. This is then replaced by a blatant attraction to men, which is awakened by Clive's introduction of Hellenic writings on same-sex relationships.

Whilst many critics have claimed that Maurice is an incarnation of Forster, he answers this question in the Terminal Note which appeared at the end of the 1960 draft of the novel:

> "In Maurice I tried to create a character who was completely unlike myself or what I supposed

> myself to be: someone handsome, healthy, bodily attractive, mentally torpid, not a bad businessman and rather a snob. Into this mixture I dropped an ingredient that puzzles him, wakes him up, torments him and finally saves him." (p. 220)

As such, we can infer that, in Maurice, Forster has not created an image of himself, but, instead, a reflection of his ideal lover. Nonetheless, the "ingredient" which torments Maurice was indeed the trait which tormented Forster: his sexuality. This is perhaps why Forster chose to end the story with Maurice eventually coming to terms with his sexuality and living happily with a companion, as Forster was never able to do so himself.

CLIVE DURHAM

Despite being members of the same college, Maurice and Clive, an upper-class gentleman in the year above Maurice, do not meet until a chance encounter when both are hoping to find their mutual friend, Risley, in his room. On this first meeting, Maurice remarks: "He was a small man – very small – with simple manners and a fair face [...] In the college he had a reputation for brains and also for exclusiveness" (p. 28). Clive is an incredibly intelligent and well-read student, who recommends that Maurice read Plato's *Symposium* instead of the books required for his degree. Early on in their friendship, Clive reveals to Maurice that he is an atheist, which Maurice finds unsettling. Nonetheless, the two soon strike up a very close bond, which leads Clive to confess his attraction Maurice. Maurice is initially disgusted, but after considering the Hellenic texts Clive suggested, he realises he loves Clive too. In this way, Clive is responsible for Maurice's first understanding of his homosexuality. Despite the distance which has developed between them by the end of the novel, Clive clearly still plays a vital role in Maurice's life, as the novel ends with Maurice announcing his new relationship with Scudder to Clive.

ALEC SCUDDER

Alec Scudder is Clive Durham's under-gamekeeper, who is due to emigrate to Argentina with his brother. As David Leavitt says in his introduction to *Maurice*, "Alec belongs to the class of guardsmen, officers and sailors with whom Forster and his friends enjoyed affairs over the years" (p. xvii). That is to say that he is of a considerably lower social class than both Maurice and Clive and, as such, Maurice dismisses him when he first encounters him. In fact, when Maurice sees Scudder (as he is referred to for the majority of the novel) for the first time, he is cavorting with two maids, kissing and teasing them. Thus, we can infer that, to use modern terminology, Scudder is probably bisexual, as he appears to have no preference between men and women. Despite their social differences, Maurice and Scudder fall into a very happy, committed relationship and the novel ends in such a way as to suggest that they live out the rest of their days happily together.

MR DUCIE

Mr Ducie is Maurice's teacher at prep-school who, in the first chapter, first introduces the notion of sex and women to Maurice. In one of the last chapters of the novel, he runs into Maurice and Scudder when they are talking in the British Museum. Fearing that his former teacher may suspect the relationship between them, Maurice gives Scudder's name and insists that he has never met Mr Ducie.

DR BARRY

Maurice's family doctor and neighbour. In the early chapters of the novel, he attends Maurice's prize-giving and asks what Maurice believes his future will look like. When, later in the novel, Maurice seeks his help to 'cure' his homosexuality, Dr Barry is horrified and sends Maurice away, urging him never to speak of the subject again.

MR LASKER JONES

Mr Lasker Jones is the final person that Maurice consults about a 'cure' for his homosexuality. He attempts to 'cure' Maurice with hypnosis, but after two sessions, he realises he cannot and suggests instead that Maurice move to a country where homosexuality is at least legal, if not accepted.

ANALYSIS

HOMOSEXUALITY AND SAME-SEX LOVE

It cannot be contested that homosexuality is the central theme of *Maurice*, as the entire narrative follows the titular character through his two most formative relationships, both of which are with members of the same sex. Although *Maurice* was not published until 1971, one year after Forster's death, he began writing this work in 1913, when homosexuality was still illegal in England and punishable by chemical castration, imprisonment and fines. It is therefore unsurprising that Forster found himself creating a new genre of writing which posed the challenge of "find[ing] the words and creat[ing] a world where this type of relationship could be realised" (Symondson, 2016). Through Maurice's two vastly different relationships, firstly with Clive Durham and secondly with Alec Scudder, Forster presents and critiques the Edwardian opinions of same-sex relationships (more specifically of those between men, as lesbian sexual acts have never been illegal in the United Kingdom) that were contemporary to the time of writing.

Maurice and Clive

Maurice's relationship with Clive Durham marks the beginning of his sexual awakening. What is perhaps most interesting about this relationship is how we see Maurice's own beliefs about homo-sexuality change and progress throughout the three years they are in a committed relationship. Initially, Maurice is appalled by Clive's profession of love:

> "Maurice was scandalized, horrified. He was shocked to the bottom of his suburban soul, and exclaimed, 'Oh, rot!' The words, the manner, were out of him before he could recall them. 'Durham, you're an Englishman. I'm another. Don't talk nonsense. I'm not offended, because I know you don't mean it, but it's the only subject absolutely beyond the limit as you know, it's the worst crime in the calendar, and you must never mention it again. Durham! a rotten notion really–" (p. 48)

This reaction may come as a surprise to the reader, as Maurice inwardly expresses an inability to "relate to [heterosexual sex]" (p. 9) when his teacher, Mr Ducie, attempts to give him a talk about women and sex. Despite this and his obvious attractions to some of his schoolfriends, Maurice seems to be relatively naïve about his own sexuality. One could infer that this is due to his 'normal' middle-class upbringing during which he has been educated, received religious instruction and no doubt come to the conclusion that heterosexuality is the only kind of union one can enjoy. Nonetheless, Maurice quickly accepts Clive's profession of love and realises that he too has homosexual feelings for Clive. This is due in part to Clive's suggestion that Maurice read Plato's *Symposium*, a text which exalts the beauty of same-sex relationships. Once they have overcome this initial obstacle, Maurice and Clive soon enter into a happy, committed relationship, despite being part of a society which would deem their love to be criminal. Nevertheless, Clive's reluctance to sexually consummate their relationship could indicate that he is torn between societal expectations and his own emotions. He is clearly incredibly fond of Maurice; he spends most of his time with him and is unafraid of showing his love through physical intimacies such as kissing and hand holding, but he insists that their relationship must remain 'platonic' in regard to sexual intercourse.

Later on in the novel, after having suffered from influenza, Clive finds himself supposedly 'cured' of his homosexuality. He tells Maurice that they must end their relationship and that he has experienced "a blind alteration of the life spirit, just an announcement, 'You who loved men, will henceforward love women. Understand it or not, it's the same to me'" (p. 103). He professes to suddenly finding homosexual relationships to be abhorrent and goes away to Greece (somewhat ironically, as it was through Greek literature that he discovered his latent homosexuality) and meets Lady Anne Woods, whom he then marries. Once could therefore deduce that, through the relationship between Maurice and Clive, Forster is exploring the effect that societal opinion can have on illicit relationships, such as those between two people of the same sex. On the one hand, obviously the illegal nature of homosexual relationships served as a deterrent for men at the time. Nonetheless, it is clear that men still entered into these relationships, as can be seen when Maurice later meets Dickie, who is unsurprised by Maurice's attraction to him:

> "The boy said nothing either. The varieties of development are endless, and it so happened that he understood the situation perfectly. If Hall insisted, he would not kick up a row, but he had rather not: he felt like that about it." (p. 130)

This apathy towards Maurice's advances suggests that it is not entirely unexpected and therefore one could infer that Dickie may have had some experience of homosexual encounters in the past; in England, homosexual relationships between public school boys have long been regarded as a normal aspect of their sexual awakening, particularly within the culture specific to boarding schools. Perhaps, therefore, Forster is highlighting this hypocrisy in public opinion through Maurice's relationship with Clive and his encounter with Dickie.

Maurice and Scudder

Maurice's second relationship in the novel is with Alec Scudder (known as Scudder throughout the majority of the novel), who is Clive's under-gamekeeper. Despite the apparent differences between their social stations, they soon form an intimate bond and the novel ultimately ends suggesting that they go on to have a happy and loving relationship *ad infinitum*. Forster explains his decision to end the novel happily in his Terminal Note, written in 1960:

> "A happy ending was imperative. I shouldn't have bothered to write otherwise. I was determined that in fiction anyway two men should fall in love and remain in it for the ever and ever that fiction allows, and in this sense Maurice and Alec still roam the greenwood. [...] If it ended unhappily, with a lad dangling from a noose or with a suicide pact, all would be well, for there is no pornography or seduction of minors. But the lovers get away unpunished and consequently recommend crime." (p. 220)

One can therefore infer from this that, as a homosexual man himself who lived in fear of persecution for loving the same sex, Forster used his fiction, specifically *Maurice*, as an outlet for his frustrated feelings. As homosexuality was only decriminalised three years before his death, it must have been very difficult for Forster to imagine a world in which homosexuality was accepted and he would be free to love another man. It is also possible that Scudder's class position feeds into the viability of their relationship; had Scudder been more educated, he may have felt more influence from society and therefore denied his homosexual tendencies. In reality, Scudder's lack of education allows him to connect with his primal urges in a way which actually suggests that he would be more likely to be called bisexual by today's standards: in a letter to Maurice after they have 'shared' (physically consummated their relationship), Scudder explains his flirtation with two maids, as witnessed by Maurice, by saying "It is natural to want a girl, you cannot go against human nature" (p. 192). Nonetheless, he never attempts to deny his sexuality to Maurice and seems to view his sexual urges as perfectly natural, although he does use its criminal status to attempt to blackmail Maurice into seeing him. However, by the end of the novel, the two have reconciled and are happily committed to each other; perhaps Forster wished to write the happy ending that he and his long-term partner could never have.

FURTHER REFLECTION

SOME QUESTIONS TO THINK ABOUT...

- For what reason do you think that Forster refrained from publishing *Maurice* during his lifetime, despite homosexuality being legalised in 1967 (three years before his death)?
- Is the 1987 film of *Maurice* (produced by Merchant Ivory) a faithful adaptation of the novel?
- In his Terminal Note, written in 1960, Forster states: "We had not realised that what the public really loathes in homosexuality is not the thing itself but having to think about it" (p.224). To what extent do you believe this influenced Forster's writing of *Maurice*, with particular reference to the lack of descriptions of the physical act of homosexual sexual intercourse?
- How is gender presented in *Maurice*? Answer with particular reference to Maurice's opinions of his sisters, mother and Clive's wife. To what

extent do you think that Maurice's opinion of women is affected by his own issues with his sexuality?

- Compare and contrast the homosexual relationships presented in *Maurice* with their heterosexual counterparts in *A Room with a View* (another work by Forster).
- Compare and contrast Maurice's relationship with Clive to his relationship with Scudder. Why do you think Forster decided to portray these two relationships in such stark contrast?
- How do the homosexual relationships portrayed in *Maurice* compare to those portrayed in more modern texts, such as *Oranges Are Not the Only Fruit* (1985) by Jeanette Winterson (English writer, born in 1959) and *Aristotle and Dante Discover the Secrets of the Universe* (2012) by Benjamin Alire Sáenz (American poet, novelist and children's author born in 1954)?
- How do the homosexual relationships portrayed in *Maurice* compare to those in earlier or contemporary texts such as *The Picture of Dorian Gray* (1890) by Oscar Wilde (Irish poet, playwright and novelist, 1854-1900)?
- What role do the themes of class and education play in *Maurice?*

We want to hear from you!
Leave a comment on your online library
and share your favourite books on social media!

FURTHER READING

REFERENCE EDITION

- Forster, E. M. (2005) *Maurice.* London: Penguin Classics.

REFERENCE STUDIES

- Symondson, K. (2016) E M Forster's gay fiction. *The British Library.* [Online]. [Accessed 11 January 2019]. Available from: <https://www.bl.uk/20th-century-literature/articles/e-m-forsters-gay-fiction>

ADAPTATIONS

- *Maurice.* (1987) [Film]. James Ivory. Dir. United Kingdom: Merchant Ivory.
- *Maurice.* (1998) [Theatre]. Roger Parsley and Andy Graham.

MORE FROM BRIGHTSUMMARIES.COM

- Reading guide – *A Passage to India* by E. M. Forster.

- Reading guide – *A Room with a View* by E. M. Forster.
- Reading guide – *Howards End* by E. M. Forster.